Carlo Acutis

His Legacy and A Powerful 9-days Novena for Everyday Miracles. The First Millennial Saint. A guided meditation

By

Fr Vincent X. Veneration

Dedication

In the name of the Father, the Son, and the Holy Spirit,

This book is lovingly dedicated to all the faithful souls who seek the extraordinary in the ordinary, and to those who, like Carlo Acutis, have ignited a spark of divine light within us all.

May your unwavering faith and devotion be a beacon of hope for generations to come, guiding us toward the path of righteousness and the profound miracles that await us on our spiritual journey.

In honor of Carlo Acutis and the legacy of love and miracles he left behind, this book is dedicated to the believers, the seekers, and the miracle-makers.

With profound gratitude and blessings,

Fr Vincent X. Veneration.

Biography

When we encounter the sanctification of a young soul, such as St. Dominic Savio or Blessed Imelda Lambertini, it may lead us to believe that such remarkable and radiant holiness belongs to the distant past. However, there's no reason why a young person in our modern age cannot follow in the footsteps of Christ with equal devotion, even while fully embracing the technology of our time, despite its temptations. Please take a moment to watch this video, as we delve into the life of Carlo Acutis, an Italian teenager who, despite being known as a 'computer geek,' has already been declared Venerable by the Church.

Carlo was born on May 3, 1991, in London, to Italian parents who relocated the family to Milan when he was just three months old. It was there that Carlo grew up, attending local schools and later a Jesuit high school. From a young age, Carlo displayed deep devotion to Our Lady. He committed to daily recitations of the Rosary and, after his first Communion at the tender age of 7, he made it a goal to receive the Eucharist daily and attend confession weekly.

Carlo's compassion and maturity were extraordinary, even as a child. In the face of bullies targeting classmates with disabilities, Carlo courageously stepped in to defend them. He also extended his support to friends enduring their parents' divorces, inviting them into his home and offering solace.

Francesca Consolini, postulator for the causes of the saints at the Archdiocese of Milan, expressed, 'He showed extraordinary care for others; he was sensitive to the problems and situations of his friends and those who lived close to him and were with him day to day.'

Carlo's warm and gentle heart mirrors the holiness of many earlier saints, but in one significant way, Carlo was unique. Living in the 21st century, he had access to computers and the internet, which he found fascinating. He perceived the media as a powerful means for Christians to evangelize and spread the Gospel.

With his friendly and tech-savvy nature, coupled with a love for technology, particularly in film and comic editing, Carlo was much like many of today's teenagers. Nevertheless, his deep love for Christ set him apart. It was this profound connection with God that sustained him through his most challenging trial—his battle with leukemia. From the moment of his diagnosis, Carlo resolved to offer all his suffering for the Church and the Pope. Even during agonizing treatments, his thoughts were with others. When asked by a doctor about his pain, Carlo replied, 'There are people who suffer much more than me.' Carlo Acutis, pray for us!

Cataloguing Eucharistic Miracles with a Website
One of his most significant computer ventures was the cataloging of Eucharistic miracles worldwide. He embarked on this project at the age of 11, writing, 'The more Eucharist we receive, the more we will become like Jesus, so that on this earth we will have a foretaste of Heaven.' He then implored his parents to take him to places of Eucharistic miracles.More than two years after the fact, the undertaking was finished.

Acutis meticulously researched '136 Eucharistic miracles that occurred over the centuries in different countries around the world and have been acknowledged by the Church,' compiling them into a virtual museum. He not only created a website to house this virtual museum but also helped create panel presentations that have traveled worldwide.

The Enduring Legacy of Carlo Acutis

Carlo Acutis has left an indelible mark on our faith. The Church of San Giuseppe in Molfetta, Italy, has already installed the first stained-glass window depicting Blessed Carlo Acutis, the 15-year-old who was beatified by Pope Francis on October 10 last year.

Furthermore, a first-class relic of Blessed Carlo Acutis has found a home in the Diocese of Brooklyn. This relic consists of hair trimmings from this remarkable young soul and is housed in the chapel at the Diocese of Brooklyn Chancery. It serves as a tangible reminder of his holiness, guiding us in our own spiritual journeys.

Day 1 – Novena in Honor of Carlo Acutis

Let us commence our Novena, invoking the Father, the Son, and the Holy Spirit. Amen.

Dear Heavenly Father,

We are grateful for the fervent testimony of the young Servant of God, Carlo Acutis, who embraced the Eucharist as the cornerstone of his life and the wellspring of his daily commitments, inspiring all to love You above all else. May he be swiftly numbered among the Blessed and Saints in Your Church.

Strengthen my Faith, nurture my Hope, and fortify my Charity, following in the footsteps of young Carlo, who now resides with You, having grown in these virtues.

(Please express your personal request here...)

We place our trust in You, Father, and in Your Beloved Son, Jesus, as well as in the intercession of the Virgin Mary, our Dearest Mother, and in the prayers of Your Servant, Carlo Acutis.

"To be always close to Jesus, that is my life's purpose."
"The Eucharist: My Pathway to Heaven."

Blessed Carlo Acutis, intercede for us!

Recite 1 Our Father, 1 Hail Mary, and 1 Glory Be...

Day 2 – Novena in Honor of Carlo Acutis

Let us begin our Novena, invoking the Father, the Son, and the Holy Spirit. Amen.

Dear Heavenly Father,

We are grateful for the fervent testimony of the young Servant of God, Carlo Acutis, who embraced the

Eucharist as the cornerstone of his life and the wellspring of his daily commitments, inspiring all to love You above all else. May he be swiftly numbered among the Blessed and Saints in Your Church.

Strengthen my Faith, nurture my Hope, and fortify my Charity, following in the footsteps of young Carlo, who now resides with You, having grown in these virtues.

(Please express your personal request here...)

We place our trust in You, Father, and in Your Beloved Son, Jesus, as well as in the intercession of the Virgin Mary, our Dearest Mother, and in the prayers of Your Servant, Carlo Acutis.

"To be always close to Jesus, that is my life's purpose."
"The Eucharist: My Pathway to Heaven."

Blessed Carlo Acutis, intercede for us!

Recite 1 Our Father, 1 Hail Mary, and 1 Glory Be...

Day 3 – Novena in Honor of Carlo Acutis

Let us commence our Novena, invoking the Father, the Son, and the Holy Spirit. Amen.

Dear Heavenly Father,

We are grateful for the fervent testimony of the young Servant of God, Carlo Acutis, who embraced the Eucharist as the cornerstone of his life and the wellspring of his daily commitments, inspiring all to love You above all else. May he be swiftly numbered among the Blessed and Saints in Your Church.

Strengthen my Faith, nurture my Hope, and fortify my Charity, following in the footsteps of young Carlo, who now resides with You, having grown in these virtues.

(Please express your personal request here...)

We place our trust in You, Father, and in Your Beloved Son, Jesus, as well as in the intercession of the Virgin Mary, our Dearest Mother, and in the prayers of Your Servant, Carlo Acutis.

"To be always close to Jesus, that is my life's purpose."
"The Eucharist: My Pathway to Heaven."

Blessed Carlo Acutis, intercede for us!

Recite 1 Our Father, 1 Hail Mary, and 1 Glory Be...

Day 4 – Novena in Honor of Carlo Acutis

Let us begin our Novena, invoking the Father, the Son, and the Holy Spirit. Amen.

Dear Heavenly Father,

We are grateful for the fervent testimony of the young Servant of God, Carlo Acutis, who embraced the

Eucharist as the cornerstone of his life and the wellspring of his daily commitments, inspiring all to love You above all else. May he be swiftly numbered among the Blessed and Saints in Your Church.

Strengthen my Faith, nurture my Hope, and fortify my Charity, following in the footsteps of young Carlo, who now resides with You, having grown in these virtues.

(Please express your personal request here...)

We place our trust in You, Father, and in Your Beloved Son, Jesus, as well as in the intercession of the Virgin Mary, our Dearest Mother, and in the prayers of Your Servant, Carlo Acutis.

"To be always close to Jesus, that is my life's purpose."
"The Eucharist: My Pathway to Heaven."

Blessed Carlo Acutis, intercede for us!

Day 5 – Novena to Carlo Acutis

Let us begin by invoking the Father, the Son, and the Holy Spirit. Amen.

Dear Heavenly Father,

We are grateful for the inspiring example of the young Servant of God, Carlo Acutis, who centered his life on the Eucharist, drawing strength from it for his daily life, encouraging all to love You above all else. May he soon be counted among the Blessed and Saints in Your Church.

May my Faith be strengthened, my Hope nurtured, and my Charity fortified, following the footsteps of young Carlo, who now resides with You, growing in these virtues.

(Share your request here...)

I place my trust in You, Father, and in Your Beloved Son, Jesus, along with the intercession of the Virgin Mary, our Dearest Mother, and Your Servant, Carlo Acutis.

"Being close to Jesus is my life plan."

"The Eucharist: My Path to Heaven."

Blessed Carlo Acutis, pray for us!

Recite 1 Our Father, 1 Hail Mary, and 1 Glory Be...

Day 6 -Novena to Carlo Acutis

Let us begin by invoking the Father, the Son, and the Holy Spirit. Amen.

Dear Heavenly Father,

We are thankful for the inspiring example of the young Servant of God, Carlo Acutis, who centered his life on the Eucharist, drawing strength from it for his daily life, encouraging all to love You above all else. May he soon be counted among the Blessed and Saints in Your Church.

May my Faith be strengthened, my Hope nurtured, and my Charity fortified, following the footsteps of young Carlo, who now resides with You, growing in these virtues.

(Share your request here...)

I place my trust in You, Father, and in Your Beloved Son, Jesus, along with the intercession of the Virgin Mary, our Dearest Mother, and Your Servant, Carlo Acutis.

"Being close to Jesus is my life plan."

"The Eucharist: My Path to Heaven."

Blessed Carlo Acutis, pray for us!

Recite 1 Our Father, 1 Hail Mary, and 1 Glory Be.

Day 7 – Novena to Carlo Acutis

Let us begin by invoking the Father, the Son, and the Holy Spirit. Amen.

Dear Heavenly Father,

We are thankful for the inspiring example of the young Servant of God, Carlo Acutis, who centered his life on the Eucharist, drawing strength from it for his daily life, encouraging all to love You above all else. May he soon be counted among the Blessed and Saints in Your Church.

May my Faith be strengthened, my Hope nurtured, and my Charity fortified, following the footsteps of young Carlo, who now resides with You, growing in these virtues.

(Share your request here...)

I place my trust in You, Father, and in Your Beloved Son, Jesus, along with the intercession of the Virgin Mary, our Dearest Mother, and Your Servant, Carlo Acutis.

"Being close to Jesus is my life plan."

"The Eucharist: My Path to Heaven."

Blessed Carlo Acutis, pray for us!

Recite 1 Our Father, 1 Hail Mary, and 1 Glory Be...

Day 8 – Novena to Carlo Acutis

Let us begin by invoking the Father, the Son, and the Holy Spirit. Amen.

Dear Heavenly Father,

We are thankful for the inspiring example of the young Servant of God, Carlo Acutis, who centered his life on the Eucharist, drawing strength from it for his daily life, encouraging all to love You above all else. May he soon be counted among the Blessed and Saints in Your Church.

May my Faith be strengthened, my Hope nurtured, and my Charity fortified, following the footsteps of young Carlo, who now resides with You, growing in these virtues.

(Share your request here...)

I place my trust in You, Father, and in Your Beloved Son, Jesus, along with the intercession of the Virgin Mary, our Dearest Mother, and Your Servant, Carlo Acutis.

"Being close to Jesus is my life plan."

"The Eucharist: My Path to Heaven."

Blessed Carlo Acutis, pray for us!

Recite 1 Our Father, 1 Hail Mary, and 1 Glory Be.

Day 9 – Novena to Carlo Acutis

Let us begin by invoking the Father, the Son, and the Holy Spirit. Amen.

Dear Heavenly Father,

We are thankful for the inspiring example of the young Servant of God, Carlo Acutis, who centered his life on the Eucharist, drawing strength from it for his daily life, encouraging all to love You above all else. May he soon be counted among the Blessed and Saints in Your Church.

May my Faith be strengthened, my Hope nurtured, and my Charity fortified, following the footsteps of young Carlo, who now resides with You, growing in these virtues.

(Share your request here...)

I place my trust in You, Father, and in Your Beloved Son, Jesus, along with the intercession of the Virgin Mary, our Dearest Mother, and Your Servant, Carlo Acutis.

"Being close to Jesus is my life plan."

"The Eucharist: My Path to Heaven."

Blessed Carlo Acutis, pray for us!

Recite 1 Our Father, 1 Hail Mary, and 1 Glory Be.

Conclusion

As we conclude our journey through Blessed Carlo Acutis' life and devotion, we are reminded that holiness knows no age or era. Carlo, a young Italian adolescent from the twenty-first century, is a shining example of unwavering faith, compassion, and a deep connection to the Eucharist.

His story dispels the myth that sanctity is a thing of the distant past. Carlo, a "computer geek" in his own words, used modern technology to spread the gospel. He saw media as a tool for evangelization, reminding us that we can enjoy the benefits of modern life while remaining rooted in our faith.

Carlo's compassion and maturity, visible even in his early years, speak of a caring heart. He stood up to bullies and offered support to classmates who were going through parental divorces. His goodness echoes the legacy of many saints before him.

Carlo, on the other hand, was not your average adolescent; he was a one-of-a-kind. His deep love for

Christ, as evidenced by his daily recitation of the Rosary and his fervent participation in the Eucharist and confession, distinguished him. This deep friendship with God saw him through his most difficult trial: his battle with leukemia.

Carlo's devotion to the Eucharist inspired him to embark on an incredible project, cataloging Eucharistic miracles all over the world. This project, which he began at the age of 11, reflects his belief that the Eucharist brings us closer to Jesus and provides a glimpse of Heaven on Earth. His dedication to this project, as well as the subsequent creation of a virtual museum to house these miracles, demonstrate his unwavering commitment.

As we conclude this novena to Carlo Acutis, we consider his words: "To always be close to Jesus, that's my life plan." He considered the Eucharist to be his "Highway to Heaven." Let us continue to be inspired by his life and pray that he will soon be counted among the Church's Blessed and Saints.

May Blessed Carlo Acutis intercede for us as we travel our own paths, always striving to be close to Jesus and relying on the Eucharist to guide and strengthen us. In

the name of the Father, Son, and Holy Spirit, Amen.
Amen. Carlo Acutis, please pray for us!

Printed in Dunstable, United Kingdom

79729251R00030